Run the Bag Up: A Hustler's Blueprint to Money Moves

Workbook

by Dory Laramore & Armand King

Walk With Me Impact Media & Education
A division of Ariginal One LLC
3960 West Point Loma Blvd. #343
San Diego, CA 92110

Walk With Me Impact
3960 West Point Loma Blvd. #343
San Diego, CA 92110

For information about special discounts for bulk
purchases please contact Walk With Me Impact
via email at: info@wwmimpact.com

ISBN: 978-1-970312-19-5

Table of Contents

Opening Statement from the Author — Dory Laramore

I come from the hustle. Born and raised in East San Diego, California, I grew up in an environment where survival came before success, and the only financial lessons I learned were the ones taught in the streets. I mastered the art of flipping money the hard way, but I paid a heavy price—nine years behind bars. When I came home, I was lost. The world had changed, and I had no blueprint for how to rebuild my life.

Then I had a realization. The same hustle, strategy, and discipline I used in the streets could be applied to something bigger—legit wealth. The difference wasn't the grind; it was where I put my energy. I took the same mindset that once had me chasing fast money and turned it into real estate investments, business ownership, and financial freedom. Today, I own multiple properties, run a successful tax business, am a two-time author and help others escape the cycle of struggle and step into financial power.

But this ain't just about me. This is about you—the ones who were never taught how to build credit, invest money, or create real generational wealth. The ones who work hard but still live check to check because nobody ever showed them another way. I wrote this workbook as a blueprint for anyone ready to break free from the system that was never built for us.

I'm here to show you that your past does not define your future. The skills you already have—the hustle, the resilience, the ability to turn nothing into something—can be redirected toward legit financial success. This workbook will give you the tools, strategies, and game to stack money, invest wisely, and build a foundation that lasts for generations.

This is your moment. Tap in, apply the knowledge, and let's get financially up—together.

Lesson 1: The Importance of Financial Literacy & Wealth Building

This lesson lays the foundation for everything to come. Use the following exercises to reflect on your current habits and build a clear vision for your financial future.

Lesson 1 Learning Objectives

By the end of this lesson, you will be able to:

- Define *financial literacy* and explain why it matters in everyday life.
- Reflect on your current money habits and identify areas for growth.
- Complete a personal money self-assessment to understand your financial baseline.
- Recognize the importance of setting clear, achievable financial goals.
- Begin building awareness of where your money goes each week and why budgeting matters.

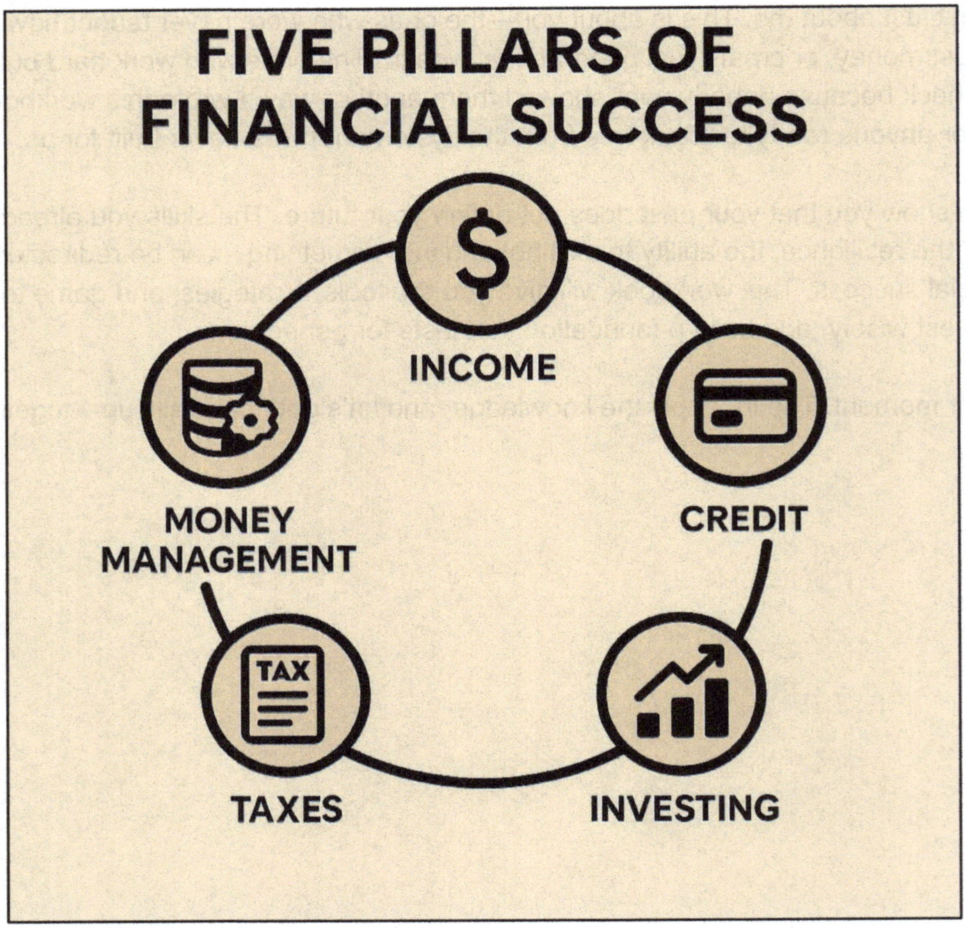

Exercise 1.1: Financial Literacy Self-Assessment

Rate your current understanding in each area on a scale of 1–5 (1 = No Knowledge, 5 = Very Confident):

Area	Your Rating (1–5)
Budgeting	
Saving	
Credit & Debt	
Investing	
Taxes & Legal Strategies	

Which area do you feel the least confident in? Why?

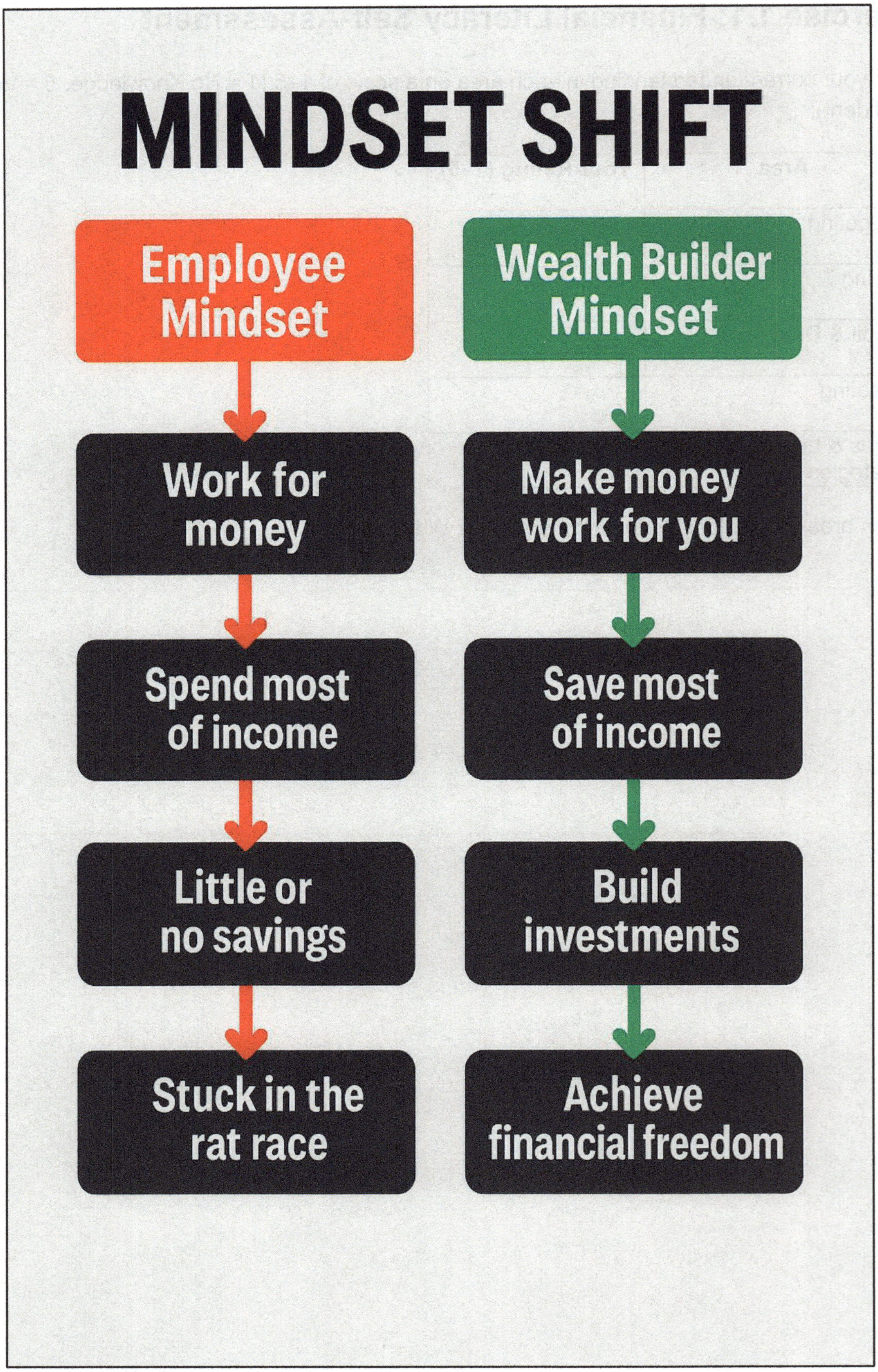
MINDSET SHIFT
Employee Mindset
Work for money
Spend most of income
Little or no savings
Stuck in the rat race
Wealth Builder Mindset
Make money work for you
Save most of income
Build investments
Achieve financial freedom

Exercise 1.2: Where Does Your Money Go?

Take a clear look at your income and spending habits.

List all your sources of income (monthly):

____

____

____

List your monthly expenses (estimates are okay):

____

____

____

What are 1–2 areas you may be overspending in?

____

____

____

Exercise 1.3: Setting SMART Financial Goals

Set clear goals using the SMART framework (Specific, Measurable, Achievable, Relevant, Time-Bound).

Short-Term Goal (3–6 months):

___

(Example: Save $500 for emergencies, Pay off a credit card)

Long-Term Goal (3–5 years):

___

(Example: Buy a home, Start a business, Invest in real estate)

What's one daily habit that can move you closer to these goals?

___

(Example: Track spending, skip eating out, set a savings reminder)

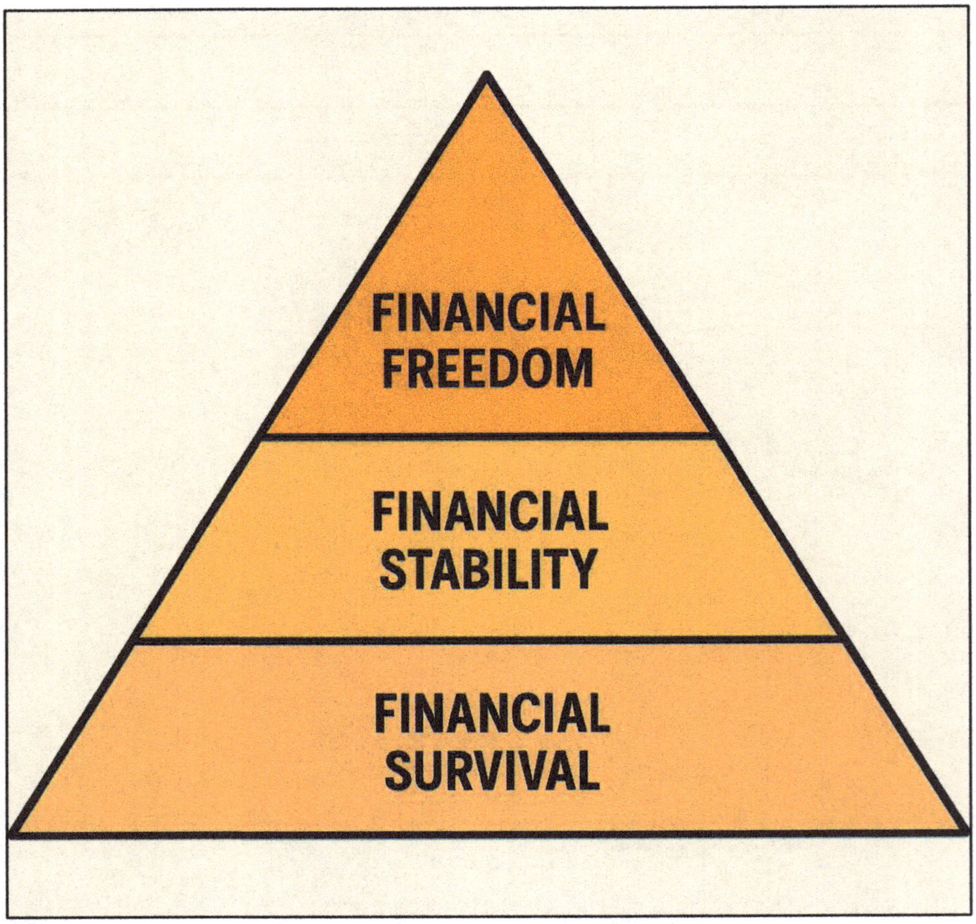

Exercise 1.4: SMART Goals Template

Short-Term Goal (Within 1 Year)

Goal Statement: What do you want to achieve in the next 12 months?

S – Specific: What exactly do you want to accomplish? Who, what, where, when, and why?

Example: I want to save $1,000 for an emergency fund.

M – Measurable: How will you track your progress? What will success look like?

Example: I will save $100 per month.

A – Achievable: Is this goal realistic with your current resources and time?

Example: Yes, I can set aside $25 per week from my paycheck.

R – Relevant: Does this goal align with your bigger financial goals and values?

Example: Yes, having an emergency fund will help me avoid credit card debt.

T – Time-Bound: What is your deadline?

Example: I will save $1,000 in 10 months.

Long-Term Goal (1–5+ Years)

Goal Statement: What do you want to achieve in 3 to 5 years or more?

S – Specific: What exactly do you want to achieve?

Example: I want to buy my first home.

M – Measurable: How much do you need? How will you measure progress?

Example: I need $20,000 for a down payment.

A – Achievable: How will you realistically reach this goal?

Example: I will save $350 per month and increase income through side hustles.

R – Relevant: Why is this goal important to you?

Example: I want to stop renting and build equity for my family's future.

T – Time-Bound: What is the target date?

Example: I want to purchase a home in 5 years.

Exercise 1.5: Weekly Expense Tracker Sheet

Week of: ______________________

Income

Source	Amount ($)
Paycheck	__________
Side Hustle	__________
Other (explain): _______	__________
Total Income	__________

Expenses by Category

Date	Category	Description	Amount ($)
	Housing (Rent, etc)		
	Food & Groceries		
	Transportation	Gas, Bus, Uber, etc	
	Utilities	Phone, Electric, etc	
	Debt Payments	Credit card, loans	
	Entertainment	Subscriptions, fun	
	Personal/Other	Clothing, hygiene, etc	
	Savings	Emergency fund, etc	

	Giving	Donations, tithes	

Summary for the Week

Item	Amount ($)
Total Income	
Total Expenses	
Amount Saved	
Leftover / Overspent	

Reflection Questions

Where did most of your money go this week?

What's one category you could spend less on?

Were you able to save anything this week? Why or why not?

What change will you make next week?

Final Takeaway

Whether you're struggling with money, just starting to learn, or already got goals—you're in the right place. This is the blueprint. And this time, we're doing it different.

Key Rule

You can't manage what you don't measure. Track your money, set your goals, and take control.

Lesson 2: The Role of Professionalism & The Hustler Mentality in Financial Success

This lesson is about how you show up and how you move. Your appearance, your discipline, your grind—it all adds up to impact your income, your relationships, and your future.

Lesson 2 Learning Objectives

By the end of this lesson, you will be able to:

- Understand how professionalism impacts opportunities, credibility, and financial success.
- Identify key traits of professionalism, including appearance, communication, punctuality, integrity, and follow-through.
- Compare and contrast the "employee mindset" with the "hustler mentality."
- Reflect on personal habits that either support or sabotage your financial goals.
- Recognize that success isn't just about what you know—but how you show up and execute daily.

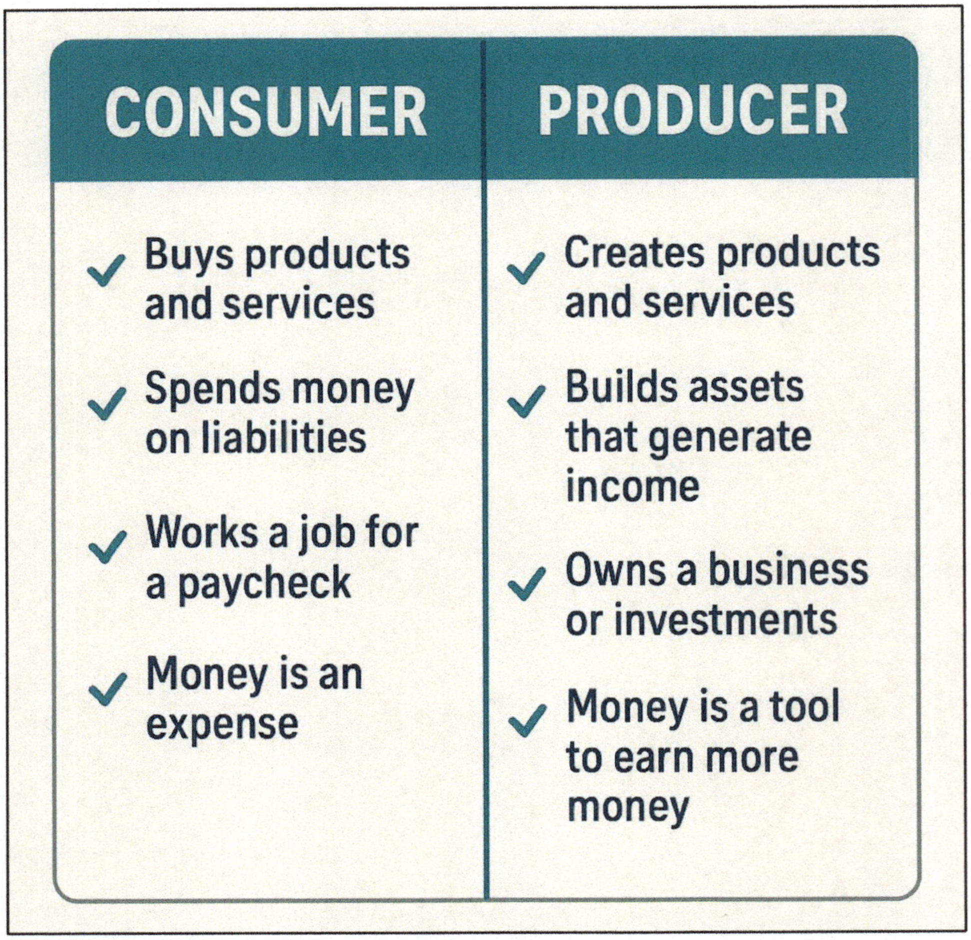

Exercise 2.1: Self-Assessment – Are You a Consumer or a Producer?

Part 1: What did you spend money on this week? List 5 items.

1. ____
2. ____
3. ____
4. ____
5. ____

Part 2: What could you create, sell, or offer to earn money this week? List 5 ideas.

1. ____
2. ____
3. ____
4. ____
5. ____

Now compare: Are you currently spending more than you're producing?

☐ Yes ☐ No ☐ About Even

Professionalism Pillars

- Appearance
- Communication
- Time Management
- Networking
- Integrity

Exercise 2.2: Professionalism Audit

Rate yourself from 1–5 (1 = Needs Work, 5 = Strong Skill):

Professional Skill	Your Rating (1–5)
Punctuality (Showing up on time)	
Communication Skills	
Networking & Relationship-Building	
Work Ethic & Consistency	
Financial Discipline	

What's one area you want to improve this month? Why?

____

____

____

____

____

Professionalism Checklist

Use this list to check yourself daily or weekly. The small things add up!

Mindset & Attitude

- Show up with a positive, can-do attitude
- Take responsibility for your actions (no blaming, no excuses)
- Stay focused on growth and learning

Appearance & Hygiene

- Clothes are clean, ironed, and appropriate for the setting
- Hair is neat and well-groomed
- Breath and body odor are checked before interacting with others
- Wear appropriate shoes and accessories (no distracting items)

Communication

- Maintain good eye contact when speaking and listening
- Speak clearly, confidently, and respectfully
- Avoid slang or profanity in professional settings
- Use proper grammar in emails and texts

Time Management

- Arrive 10 minutes early for appointments
- Stick to deadlines or communicate ahead of time if you need more
- Plan out your day with a task list or calendar

Follow-Through

- Send a follow-up email or thank you after meetings/interviews
- Keep your word—if you say you'll do something, do it
- Respond to messages within 24–48 hours

Relationship Building

- Greet people professionally (firm handshake, smile, "Nice to meet you")
- Network and introduce yourself with confidence
- Show respect to all levels of staff—no one is "beneath" you

Integrity & Accountability

- Don't lie, steal, or cheat—be trustworthy at all times
- Own up to mistakes and fix them quickly
- Keep confidential info private

Exercise 2.3: Building a Hustler Mentality

What is one hustle or income idea that fits your skills or interests?

____

____

What would it take to get started? (List tools, time, knowledge needed):

____

____

____

Action step: What's one small move you'll make this week toward that hustle?

____

____

____

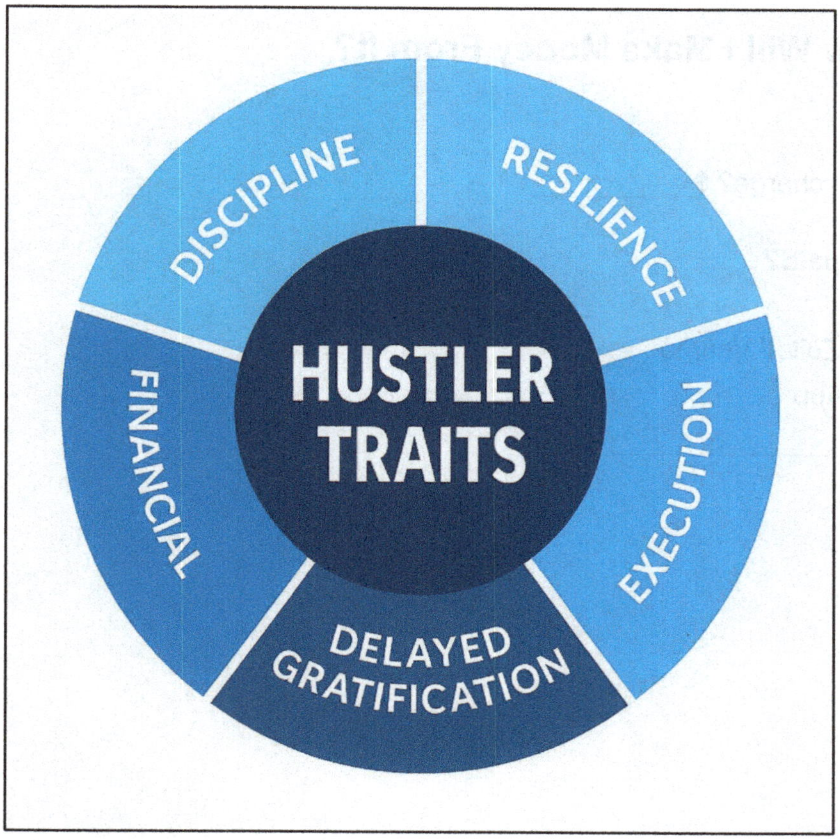

Exercise 2.4: My Producer Plan

Turn your skills, ideas, or passions into income.

Step 1: What Can I Create or Offer?

Product or Service Idea (e.g., t-shirts, digital art, tutoring, baked goods, photography, mobile car wash, etc.).

____

____

____

Step 2: Who Needs This?

Target audience – Who will buy it (e.g., teens, parents, business owners, students, etc.).

____

____

____

Step 3: How Will I Make Money From It?

Pricing Idea:

How much will I charge? $__________

How will I get paid?

☐ Cash
☐ Cash App / Zelle / Venmo
☐ Website or App
☐ Other: ____________________

Step 4: What Do I Need to Start?

Item or Tool Needed	Already Have It? (✓)	Where to Get It

Step 5: Next 3 Action Steps

What can I do this week to get it started?

1. ____

____

2. ____

____

3. ____

____

Step 6: How Will I Promote It?

☐ Word of Mouth
☐ Social Media
☐ Flyers / Business Cards
☐ Friends & Family
☐ Online Marketplace (Etsy, OfferUp, etc.)
☐ Other: ____________________

Step 7: Producer Commitment

I commit to taking action on this idea and making it real.

Signature: ________________________ **Date:** ___________

Final Takeaway

Professionalism gets your foot in the door. Hustler mentality kicks it open. Both are needed to build wealth and stand out—whether you're on a job, running your own business, or just getting started.

Key Rule

Show up like you already made it, and work like you're still trying to get there.

Lesson 3: The Foundation of Financial Success – Budgeting & Saving

This lesson helps you take control of your money. Learn to track what comes in, what goes out, and how to make saving a habit—not a hope.

Lesson 3 Learning Objectives

By the end of this lesson, you will be able to:

- Understand the importance of budgeting and saving as the cornerstones of financial stability.
- Identify and categorize your income, fixed expenses, and variable expenses.
- Apply the 50/30/20 budgeting method to your own monthly finances.
- Learn and commit to the "Pay Yourself First" strategy to prioritize savings.

Exercise 3.1: Income vs. Expenses Breakdown

Monthly Income Sources:
(List all sources like jobs, side hustles, benefits, etc.)

1. ______________________________

2. ______________________________

3. ______________________________

Total Monthly Income: $______________

Monthly Fixed Expenses:
(Things that stay the same every month – rent, car payment, etc.)

1. ______________________________

2. ______________________________

3. ______________________________

Total Fixed Expenses: $______________

Monthly Variable Expenses:
(Things that change – groceries, gas, entertainment, etc.)

1. ______________________________

2. ______________________________

3. ______________________________

Total Variable Expenses: $______________

Where can you reduce or cut back?

____

____

____

Exercise 3.2: The 50/30/20 Budgeting Challenge

Enter your current monthly income: $______________

Break it down using the 50/30/20 Rule:

- Essentials (Needs – 50%): $______________
- Savings/Debt/Investing (Growth – 30%): $______________
- Lifestyle (Wants – 20%): $______________

What's one expense you will reduce or cut this week?
(Example: Cancel a subscription, eat out less, walk instead of drive)

____

____

50/30/20 Rule
50%
Needs
Essentials you must pay for
30%
Wants
Non-essentials and fun
20%
Savings
Future financial goals
OF AFTER-TAX INCOME

Exercise 3.3: The "Pay Yourself First" Strategy

How much will you save each week starting now? $______________

Where will you put this money?

☐ High-Yield Savings Account
☐ Investment Account
☐ Emergency Fund
☐ Other: ________________________

What day of the week will you commit to making this transfer?

☐ Monday ☐ Wednesday ☐ Friday ☐ Other: ____________

Final Takeaway

Money management is the difference between surviving and thriving. When you budget with purpose and save with discipline, you start building the habits that create financial freedom.

Key Rule
Budget your money before your money budgets you.

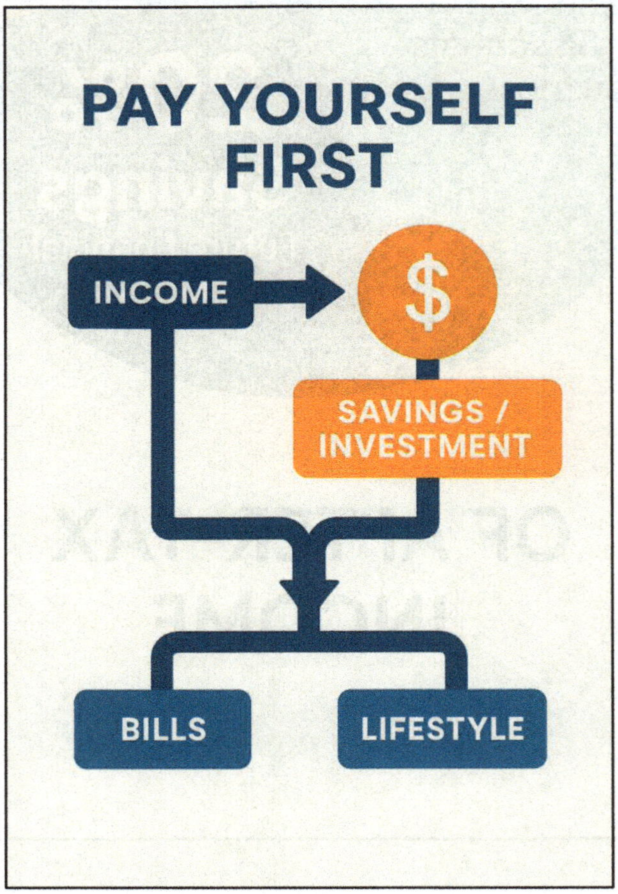

Lesson 4: Understanding Credit – The Key to Financial Leverage

Your credit score is more than just a number—it's a financial key. This lesson helps you understand how credit works, how to fix it if it's broken, and how to use it to unlock opportunities.

Lesson 4 Learning Objectives

By the end of this lesson, you will be able to:

- Understand what a credit score is, how it's calculated, and why it matters.
- Access and review your own credit report to identify key areas for improvement.
- Calculate your credit utilization and develop a plan to lower it if necessary.
- Identify credit-building tools such as secured credit cards, credit-builder loans, or authorized user status.
- Create a basic credit repair strategy using proven repayment methods.

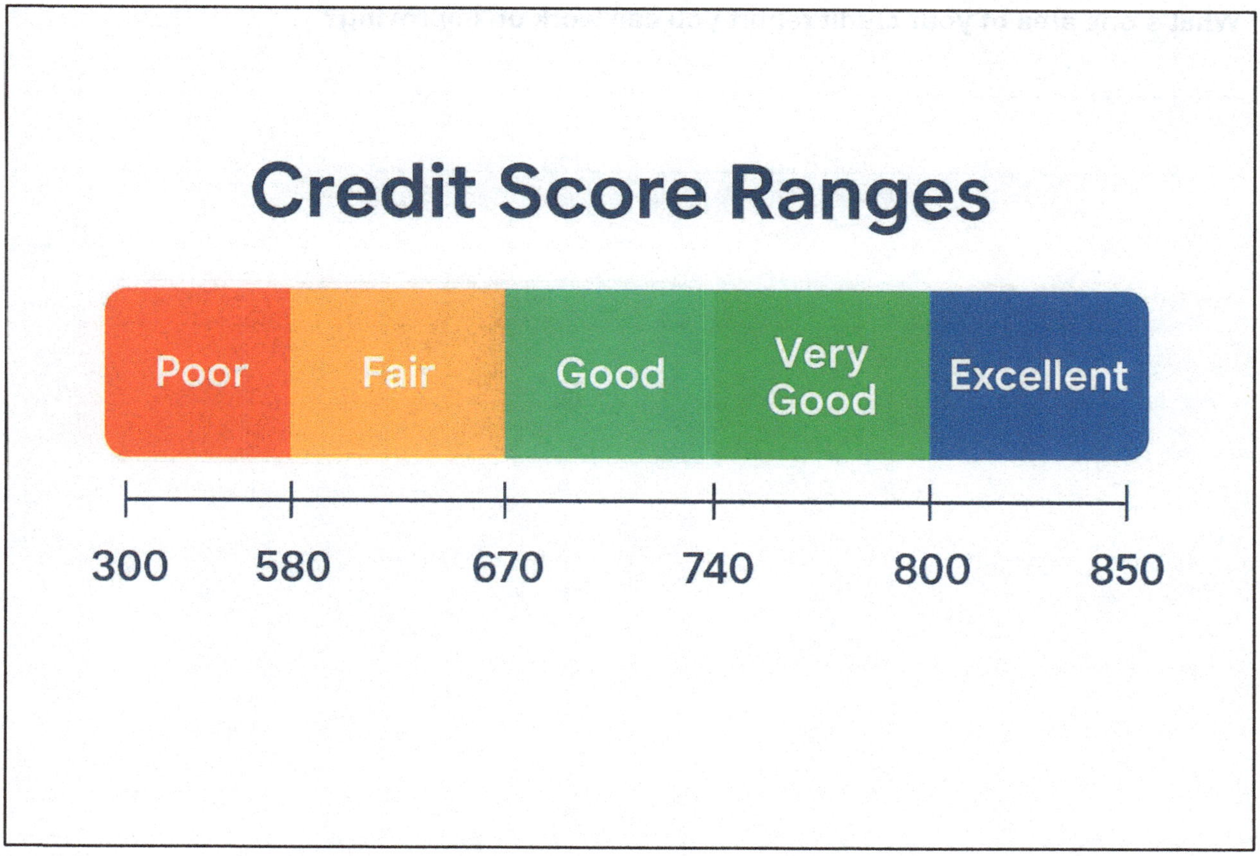

Exercise 4.1: Check & Analyze Your Credit Report

Step 1: Visit AnnualCreditReport.com and download your free report.

Step 2: Review your information and fill in the details below:

Credit Score (if available): ___________

Number of open credit accounts: ___________

Any negative marks? (late payments, collections, etc.):

What's one area of your credit report you can work on improving?

Exercise 4.2: Credit Utilization Calculator

List each credit card you have:

Credit Card Name	Limit ($)	Current Balance ($)

Total Credit Limit: $______________

Total Balance Owed: $______________

Utilization Rate: (Balance ÷ Limit) x 100 = ________%

Goal: Keep credit utilization below 30% (Ideal = Under 10%)

Action Step: If over 30%, how much do you need to pay down to reach that threshold?

$______________

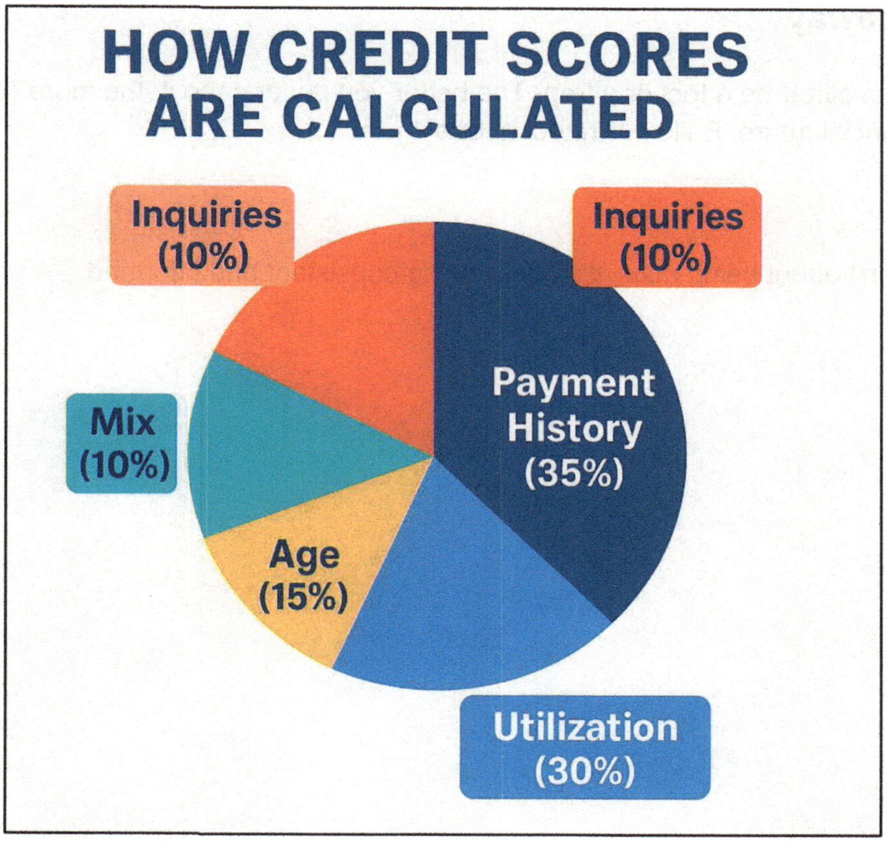

Exercise 4.3: Credit Repair Action Plan

List any debts, collections, or credit issues below:

Debt/Account Name	Balance Owed	Status (Current, Late, Collection)

What's your repayment strategy?

☐ Pay smallest balances first (snowball method)
☐ Pay highest-interest debts first (avalanche method)
☐ Negotiate pay-for-delete with collections
☐ Set up auto-pay for all bills

Are you building credit? Choose one to begin with:

☐ Secured Credit Card
☐ Credit-Builder Loan
☐ Authorized User on Trusted Account

Final Takeaway

Your credit can either be a tool or a trap. The better you understand it, the more control you gain over your financial future. Build it. Protect it. Use it wisely.

Key Rule

Good credit isn't about being rich—it's about being consistent and informed.

Lesson 5: Creating Multiple Streams of Income & Developing an Investor's Mindset

Millionaires don't rely on one income stream—they build multiple. This lesson helps you shift your mindset and take steps toward creating income that works for you, even when you're not working.

Lesson 5 Learning Objectives

By the end of this lesson, you will be able to:

- Explain the importance of having more than one income stream for financial security and wealth building.
- Distinguish between assets and liabilities in your personal spending habits.
- Identify at least one new income stream you are interested in developing.
- Begin researching an investment option and outline a first step toward participation.
- Use a structured worksheet to brainstorm income ideas based on your skills, interests, and real-life opportunities.

Exercise 5.1: Income Stream Self-Assessment

How many income streams do you currently have?

List them below:

1.

2.

3.

What additional income stream would you like to start next?

Why did you choose that one?

Exercise 5.2: Identify Assets vs. Liabilities

List 3 things you recently spent money on:

1. ______________________________

2. ______________________________

3. ______________________________

For each item, ask yourself:

- Was it an asset (something that puts money in your pocket) or a liability (takes money out)?
- Could that money have gone into something that makes you money instead?

Reflection: How could you have used one of those purchases to invest instead?

____

____

____

____

____

Exercise 5.3: Investment Exploration

Choose one area to research this week:

☐ Stocks ☐ Real Estate ☐ Business ☐ Digital Product ☐ Other: ____________

What did you learn from your research?

What is one small action you can take to begin?

(Example: Open a free investment app, explore real estate in your area, outline a digital product idea.)

Exercise 5.4: Income Stream Brainstorming Sheet

Objective

Use this worksheet to discover new ways to make money by tapping into your skills, interests, and experience.

Section 1: Skills Inventory

List 3–5 things you're good at or have experience in.

Skill #1: ______________________________

Skill #2: ______________________________

Skill #3: ______________________________

Skill #4: ______________________________

Skill #5: ______________________________

Section 2: Interests & Passions

List the things you enjoy doing or learning about.

Interest #1: ______________________________

Interest #2: ______________________________

Interest #3: ______________________________

Section 3: What People Ask You For Help With

"If people already value your help, there's a business there."

What People Ask You For Help With

Think about what people come to you for advice or help with.

____

____

____

Section 4: Hustle Ideas Based on Your Answers

Remember: No idea is too small. Many six-figure businesses started with just one skill and one audience.

Hustle Ideas Based on Your Answers

Combine your skills, interests, and what people ask you for to create possible income stream ideas.

Idea #1: ______________________________

Idea #2: ______________________________

Idea #3: ______________________________

Section 5: Income Model Type

Label each idea as:

- Active (trading time for money)
- Semi-Passive (some upfront effort, then it runs itself)
- Passive (money works for you)

Hustle Idea	Type (Active, Semi-Passive, Passive)

Section 6: Choose One to Start

Which idea are you going to start exploring?

What are the first 3 steps to get this off the ground?

1.

2.

3.

Final Takeaway

You don't need to be rich to start investing—you need to start investing to get rich. One income stream is survival. Multiple streams are freedom. Build smart. Build steady. Build wealth.

Key Rule

Don't just work for money—make your money work for you.

Employee vs. Investor Mindset

Employee Mindset	Investor Mindset
Strives for job security	Strives for financial freedom
Earns a paycheck	Grows money into income
Works to build someone else's business	Works to build own assets
Spends now, saves later	Saves now, spends later
Relies on one source of income	Has multiple streams of income
Prives for financial freedom	Has multiple streams of income

accnoact.os

Lesson 6: How to Buy a Car Without Going Broke

A car can be a necessary tool—or a financial trap. This lesson helps you make smart vehicle decisions that support your goals instead of draining your pockets.

Lesson 6 Learning Objectives

By the end of this lesson, you will be able to:

- Understand the true long-term cost of vehicle ownership, including depreciation, interest, insurance, and maintenance.
- Compare different auto loan interest rates and calculate how credit score impacts total cost.
- Evaluate the pros and cons of buying vs. leasing based on personal goals and financial situation.
- Make informed decisions when shopping for a vehicle by considering affordability, purpose, and alignment with long-term wealth goals.
- Commit to a strategy that supports smart car ownership without compromising financial health.

Exercise 6.1: True Cost of Ownership Calculation

Choose a car you're interested in (real or hypothetical) and estimate the total cost over 5 years.

- **Car Make/Model:** ____

- **Purchase Price:** $__________________

- **Loan Interest (Estimate):** $__________________

- **Depreciation (Approx. 50% over 5 years):** $__________________

- **Insurance & Maintenance:** $__________________

Total 5-Year Cost Estimate: $__________________

Reflection: Does this car support your financial goals—or stretch your budget too far?

____

____

Exercise 6.2: Auto Loan Interest Rate Impact

Compare the cost of borrowing at different interest rates.

- **Loan Amount:** $20,000
- **Term:** 5 years

Interest Rate	Estimated Monthly Payment	Total Interest Paid
3%	$______________	$______________
10%	$______________	$______________

Difference in Interest Paid: $______________

Lesson: A higher credit score = less money wasted on interest.

Exercise 6.3: Buying vs. Leasing Breakdown

Option	Pros	Cons
Buying	______________________	______________________
Leasing	______________________	______________________

Which option fits your current goals and financial situation? Why?

____

____

____

Final Takeaway

A car should move you forward in life—not hold you back financially. Know the full cost, stick to your budget, and always drive something that serves your wealth—not your ego.

Key Rule

Buy what you need, not what impresses people who don't pay your bills.

Lesson 7: How to Make Your Money Work for You

Investing is how you stop trading time for money. This lesson breaks down the basics and helps you take your first real step toward building long-term wealth through smart investments.

Lesson 7 Learning Objectives

By the end of this lesson, you will be able to:

- Understand the core concept of investing as a path to financial growth and time freedom.
- Recognize the power of compound interest and how consistent investing builds wealth over time.
- Identify different types of investment vehicles (e.g., index funds, ETFs, individual stocks) and their basic functions.
- Develop a personalized beginner investment plan, including goal setting, monthly contribution amount, and selected platform or app.
- Overcome common fears or misconceptions about investing and take the first actionable step toward becoming an investor.

INVESTMENT MINDSET: TRADER VS. INVESTOR

TRADER	INVESTOR
Short-term mindset	Long-term mindset
Quick profits	Building wealth
Buy & sell frequently	Buy & hold assets
Time the market	Grow with the morket
Focus on stock prices	Focus on company value
Stress & risk	Stability & compounding

Exercise 7.1: Investing Self-Assessment

Do you currently invest?

☐ Yes ☐ No

If not, what's holding you back?

What is one financial goal you want investing to help you achieve?
(Example: Retire early, buy a home, build generational wealth)

Exercise 7.2: Investment Growth Calculator

Use an online compound interest calculator (like investor.gov or nerdwallet.com) to estimate growth.

If you invest $100 per month with an average 8% annual return:

- In 10 years: $________________
- In 20 years: $________________
- In 30 years: $________________

What did this reveal about the power of consistent investing?

____

____

____

____

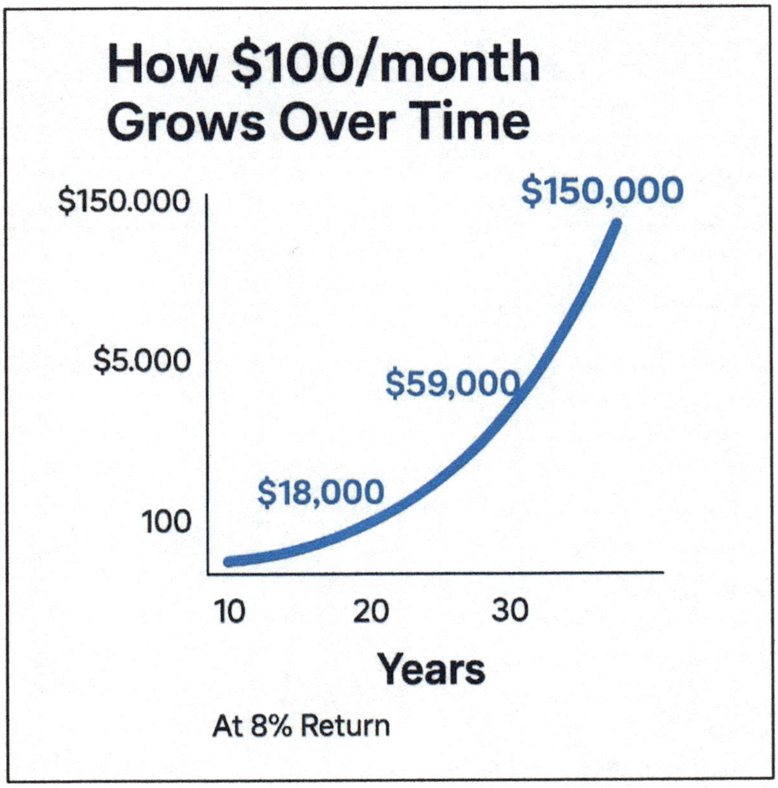

Exercise 7.3: Create Your First Investment Plan

Which type of investment will you start with?

☐ Index Fund ☐ ETF ☐ Individual Stock ☐ Other: __________

What app or brokerage will you use to invest? (Example: Fidelity, Robinhood, E-Trade, TD Ameritrade)

How much will you invest each month to start?

$_________________

When will you start? (Choose a specific date):

Final Takeaway

You don't need to be rich to invest—investing is how you get rich. Start small. Stay consistent. Watch your money grow while you sleep.

Key Rule

The best time to plant a tree was 20 years ago. The second best time is today.

Lesson 8 Workbook: Turning Your Ideas into Income

Starting your own business is one of the fastest ways to build wealth, create freedom, and take control of your future. This lesson helps you take that first step—from idea to income.

Lesson 8 Learning Objectives

By the end of this lesson, you will be able to:

- Select and refine one business idea from your Lesson 5 brainstorming session, defining the specific problem it solves and identifying a target first customer.
- Create a lean startup cost estimate for your chosen idea and identify funding gaps or opportunities to start with minimal investment.
- Develop an actionable plan for your first sale, including setting a price, selecting a promotion method, and listing specific people to contact.
- Synthesize your refined idea into a one-page business plan that outlines your mission, target market, revenue model, and immediate action steps.
- Apply a hustler's mindset to anticipate challenges and distinguish between strategically pivoting and quitting when faced with obstacles.

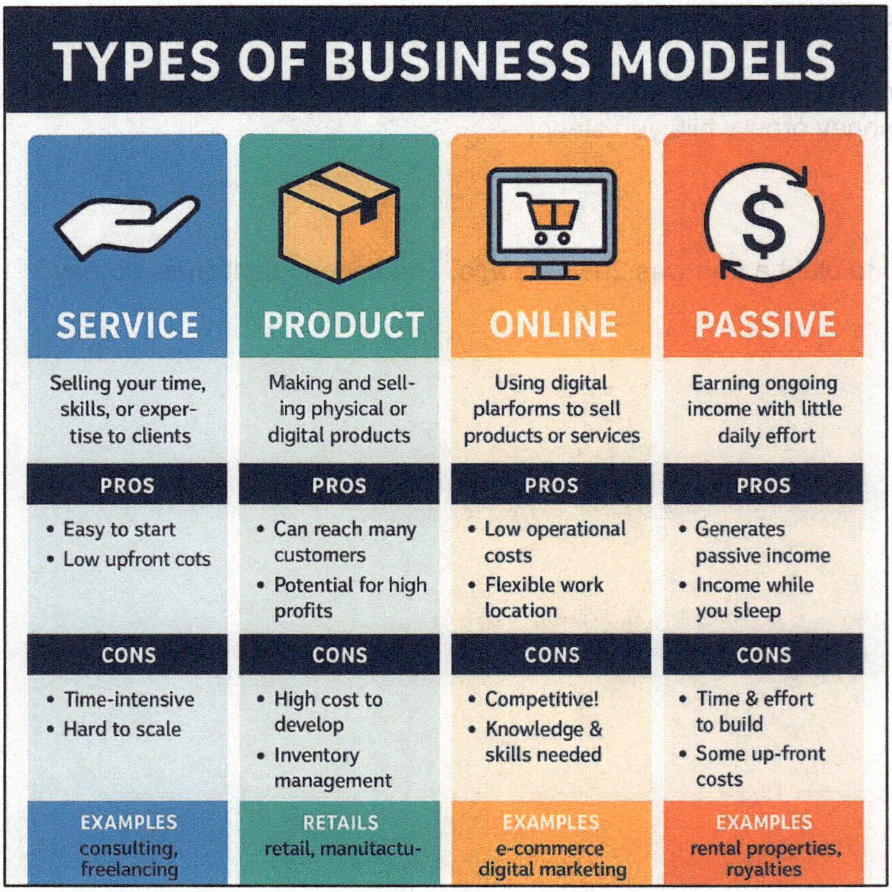

Exercise 8.1: Select & Refine Your Business Idea

What was the top idea from your Lesson 5 brainstorm?

Why did this stand out to you?

What specific problem does this idea solve for a customer? (Be precise. Instead of "people need clothes," think "young professionals in my area need affordable, stylish alterations for workwear.")

Who is the ONE specific person I imagine as my first customer? (e.g., "My friend Alex who always complains about..." or "Local salon owners who...")

What's the simplest version of this I could launch with? (e.g., "I don't need a full clothing line, just 5 custom T-shirt designs.")

Exercise 8.2: Business Cost Estimation

What do you need to launch your idea? List all expenses you expect. (Examples: License fees, supplies, website, marketing, equipment)

Item or Service Needed	Estimated Cost

Total startup cost estimate: $________________

How much can you self-fund right now? $________________

How much do you still need to raise or fund? $________________

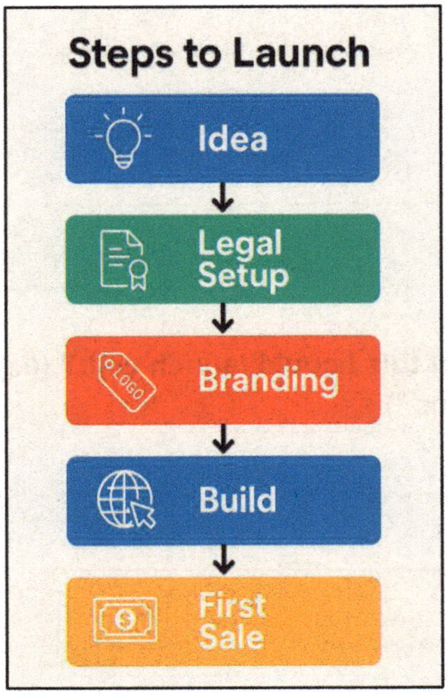

Exercise 8.3: First Sale Challenge

Your challenge this week is to get your first customer—no matter how small.

Describe your product or service briefly:

___

What price will you charge? $__________________

How will you promote it or share it?

- ☐ Social Media
- ☐ Word of Mouth
- ☐ Text/DM
- ☐ Email
- ☐ Other: ________________________

List 5 specific people you can reach out to today to offer your product/service:

1. ___
2. ___
3. ___
4. ___
5. ___

Exercise 8.4: One-Page Business Plan Template

Business Name:

Date Started:

1. Mission Statement

What's your purpose? What problem are you solving or value are you adding?

2.Target Market

Who are your customers? Age, location, interest, income level, etc.

3. Revenue Model

How will you make money? (Product sales, services, subscriptions, digital downloads, etc.)

4. Marketing Plan

How will people hear about you? Social media, flyers, referrals, website, etc.

____

____

____

____

____

5. Startup Needs

What do you need to get started? (Supplies, equipment, licenses, budget, etc.)

____

____

____

____

6. 3 Action Steps This Month

What are your first three steps to launch?

1. ____

____

2. ____

____

3. ____

____

Exercise 8.5: Hustler Mindset Reflection – Pivot or Quit?

Objective:

Understand the difference between giving up and shifting strategy—and how real hustlers know when to adapt.

1. What's the challenge you're facing right now?
(Example: Not getting sales, people aren't responding, lack of motivation)

2. Have you given it your best effort?

- Have you tried different approaches?
- Have you sought advice or feedback?
- Have you stayed consistent over time?

3. What's not working—and why?

Be honest. Is it the strategy, the product, the audience, or your discipline?

4. What would a pivot look like?

(Example: Switch platforms, change your offer, adjust your audience, rebrand)

5. If you quit, what will you learn from this experience?

Not all quitting is failure—only if you walk away with nothing gained.

Final Question: Is it time to PIVOT or QUIT—with a plan? Why?

Remember: Hustlers don't quit when it's hard—they adapt when it's smart.

Final Takeaway

You started with a brainstorm of possibilities in Lesson 5. In this lesson, you took one of those ideas and built a concrete, actionable plan around it. This is the process: Generate, Select, Plan, Execute. Progress over perfection.

Key Rule

Progress over perfection. Your first sale matters more than a perfect plan.

Lesson 9: Turning Your Hustle into a Legacy

Entrepreneurship isn't just about making money—it's about building something that lasts. Whether you're just starting or already hustling, this lesson will help you level up your mindset and actions.

Lesson 9 Learning Objectives

By the end of this lesson, you will be able to:

- Analyze feedback from your initial sales attempt to inform the ongoing development of your business.
- Develop a basic brand identity (name, visual style, messaging) to create professionalism and trust.
- Create simple systems for generating repeat business, gathering customer feedback, and tracking growth.
- Articulate a clear vision for the long-term community and family impact of their business (their legacy).

Exercise 9.1: Analyze Your First Sale

Look back at your First Sale Challenge from Lesson 8. What happened? Did you make contact? What did people say?

____

____

____

____

____

What was the most important thing you learned? About your customer? Your price? Your offer? How you communicated?

____

____

____

Based on this, what is one thing you will...

1. **CHANGE?** (e.g., your price, your target customer, how you describe it)

2. **KEEP DOING?** (e.g., the core service, posting on a certain platform)

3. **STOP DOING?** (e.g., a confusing part of your offer, reaching out to the wrong group)

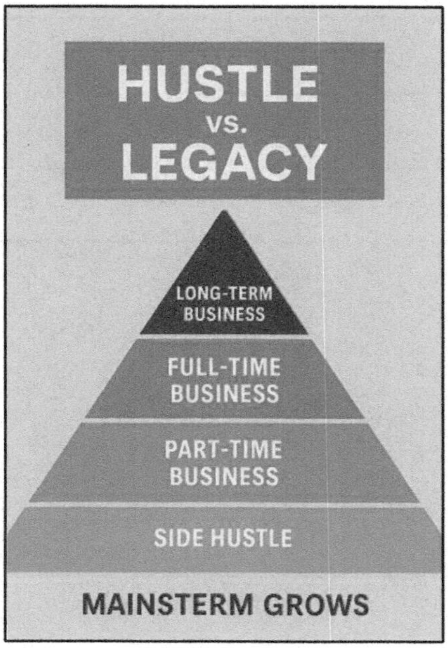

Exercise 9.2: Business Name & Branding

What name will you use for your business?

What does this name communicate to customers?

Brand Elements:

Colors you want to use:

Logo idea or concept:

What feeling or message should your brand give people?

Exercise 9.3: Build Your Customer System

1. Feedback System: How will you ask your first few customers for a testimonial or review? (Example: A text after the service: "Hey, would you mind telling me in one sentence what you liked?")

2. Repeat Business System: What can you do to encourage a customer to come back or refer a friend? (Example: A "Next Time 10% Off" card, a simple referral discount.)

3. Tracking System: What simple tool(s) will you use to track your customers, sales, or expenses? (Example: A notes page, a free Google Sheet, a notebook.)

Exercise 9.4: Define Your Legacy Impact

What is the deeper impact you want your business to have?

For your family? (Example: Create stable income, pay for education, buy a home, teach entrepreneurial skills.)

For your community? (Example: Solve a local problem, employ neighbors, inspire others, donate a portion of profits.)

In one sentence, what is the true "legacy" you are building with your work?

Lesson 10: Turning Rent Payments into Homeownership

Buying your first home is one of the most important financial decisions you'll ever make. This lesson helps you understand how to prepare, what to expect, and how to avoid costly mistakes.

Lesson 10 Learning Objectives

By the end of this lesson, you will be able to:

- Assess your current financial readiness for homeownership by evaluating credit score, income stability, debt levels, and savings habits.
- Use mortgage calculators to estimate home affordability and monthly payments, ensuring you stay within a realistic budget.
- Identify key steps in the homebuying preparation process, including credit improvement, debt reduction, saving for a down payment, and getting pre-approved.
- Create a 1- to 2-year personalized plan for becoming a first-time homebuyer, including savings goals and action items.

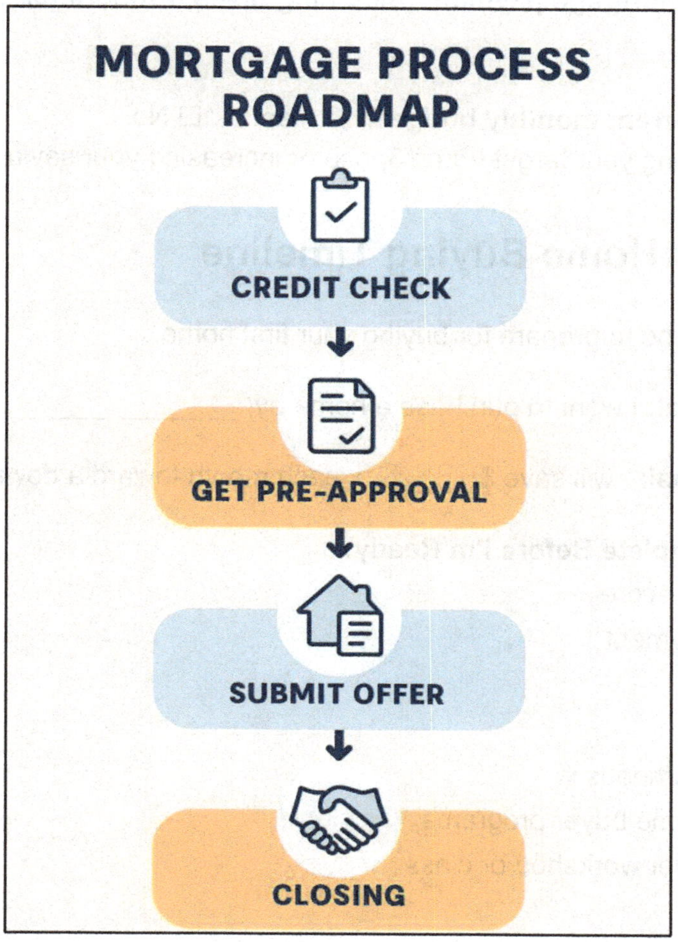

Exercise 10.1: Home Buying Readiness Test

What is your current credit score? ________________

Do you have stable income (2+ years)? ☐ Yes ☐ No

What's your estimated monthly debt (loans, credit cards, etc.)? $________________

How much can you realistically save each month toward a down payment?
$________________

Exercise 10.2: Mortgage Cost Estimation

Use an online mortgage calculator (Zillow, Bankrate, NerdWallet) to complete:

Estimated home price you'd like to buy: $________________

Estimated down payment you can afford (ex: 5%, 10%): $________________

Estimated monthly mortgage payment (including taxes & insurance):
$________________

Does this fit your current monthly budget? ☐ Yes ☐ No
(If no, consider reducing your target home 3price or increasing your savings plan.)

Exercise 10.3: Home Buying Timeline

Create a simple timeline to prepare for buying your first home.

1-Year or 2-Year Goal: I want to purchase a home by: ________________________

Monthly Savings Goal: I will save $________ each month toward a down payment.

Steps I Need to Complete Before I'm Ready:

☐ Improve my credit score
☐ Save for down payment
☐ Reduce debt
☐ Get pre-approved
☐ Research neighborhoods
☐ Learn about first-time buyer programs
☐ Attend a homebuyer workshop or class

Lesson 11: Using Real Estate to Build Long-Term Wealth

Real estate is one of the most proven ways to build long-term wealth, especially for those coming from limited means. This lesson walks you through the why, the how, and the strategies to make real estate a part of your financial journey.

Lesson 11 Learning Objectives

By the end of this lesson, participants will be able to:

- Understand the fundamentals of rental property investing, including cash flow, mortgage costs, taxes, insurance, and maintenance.
- Evaluate rental property opportunities using a basic cash flow calculator to determine if a property generates profit.
- Compare real estate markets across multiple locations by analyzing factors like home prices, rent averages, job growth, and crime levels.
- Develop a personalized 3-year investment plan by identifying a target property type, preferred strategy (e.g., buy & hold, house hacking), and savings goals for a down payment.

Exercise 11.1: Rental Property Cash Flow Calculator

Find a rental property listing online (Zillow, Redfin, or Realtor.com) and complete the fields below:

- **Property Address:** ________________________________
- **Estimated Monthly Rent:** $________________
- **Mortgage Payment:** $________________
- **Taxes:** $________________
- **Insurance:** $________________
- **Maintenance Budget (estimate 5-10%):** $________________

Monthly Cash Flow = Rent – (Mortgage + Taxes + Insurance + Maintenance)
= $________________

Does the rent cover all the expenses with profit left over? ☐ Yes ☐ No

Exercise 11.2: Real Estate Market Research

Choose **3 cities or neighborhoods** and fill out the table:

City/Neighborhood	Average Home Price	Avg. Rent	Job Growth	Crime Level

What trends do you notice?

Which city seems like the best investment opportunity right now and why?

Exercise 11.3: Create Your 3-Year Real Estate Investment Plan

How much can you save per year toward a down payment? $____________ per year

Real estate strategy you plan to start with:

☐ Buy & Hold ☐ House Hacking ☐ Fix & Flip ☐ Short-Term Rentals ☐ REITs

What type of property do you want to buy first?

☐ Single-Family ☐ Multi-Family ☐ Condo ☐ Other: ____________

Goal: I want to purchase my first property by: ________________ (Month/Year)

Final Takeaway

Real estate investing isn't just for the rich—it's for the ready. Start with knowledge. Run the numbers. Buy smart, not just fast. Your first property might not be your dream property, but it could open the door to your dream future.

Key Rule

Don't just pay rent—own assets that pay you back.

Lesson 12: Understanding Taxes to Keep More of Your Money

Understanding taxes is a game-changer for building wealth. You can't avoid paying taxes—but you can avoid overpaying them. This lesson teaches you how to keep more of your money legally through smart planning.

Lesson 12 Learning Objectives

By the end of this lesson, participants will be able to:

- Understand the role taxes play in financial planning and wealth building.
- Identify their tax bracket and determine if they are maximizing deductions and credits.
- Explore common tax-saving tools such as retirement contributions, business write-offs, and tax credits.
- Learn how a side hustle or small business can legally reduce taxable income.
- Develop a basic tax strategy to reduce overpayments and improve long-term financial outcomes.

Exercise 12.1: Tax Reality Check

What is your current income? $____________

Do you know your tax bracket? ☐ Yes ☐ No

Are you claiming the **standard deduction** or **itemizing**?

☐ Standard ☐ Itemized ☐ Not Sure

Reflection: Have you been using tax tools (credits, deductions, business write-offs) to reduce your taxes?

☐ Yes ☐ No ☐ A little bit

What's one thing you've learned so far that could help lower your taxes next year?

____

____

____

____

____

____

____

Exercise 12.2: Deductions & Credits Finder

Check all that currently apply to you:

Deductions:

☐ Student Loan Interest
☐ Mortgage Interest
☐ Medical Expenses
☐ Retirement Contributions (Traditional IRA/401(k))
☐ Home Office or Business Expenses

Credits:

☐ Child Tax Credit
☐ Education Credit (American Opportunity or Lifetime Learning)
☐ Earned Income Tax Credit
☐ Energy-Efficient Home Improvements

Total Checked: ______

Next Step: Pick 1 deduction or credit from above and research how to qualify or increase it next year.

Exercise 12.3: Start a Tax-Smart Side Hustle Plan

Even a small business can open big tax advantages.

Do you currently have a side hustle or business?

☐ Yes ☐ No ☐ Not yet, but planning

List 3 expenses you could potentially write off if your hustle was official:

1. ______________________________

2. ______________________________

3. ______________________________

Choose one step to get more tax-savvy with your business:

☐ Track business income & expenses
☐ Set up an LLC
☐ Open a business bank account
☐ Talk to a tax professional

Exercise 12.4: Retirement Account Impact

Choose one of the retirement options below and answer:

- Traditional IRA ☐
- Roth IRA ☐
- 401(k) ☐
- HSA (Health Savings Account) ☐

How much could you contribute monthly to this account? $___________

When would you like to open or increase contributions to this account?

☐ This month ☐ This year ☐ Next year

Final Takeaway

If you don't learn tax rules, you'll keep losing money by default. Tax-smart people don't make more money—they keep more of what they make.

Key Rule

Learn the system. Use the system. Don't be played by the system.

Lesson 13: Save, Stack, Invest, Flip, Repeat

Wealth isn't built overnight—it's built through habits. This lesson gives you a blueprint to turn small steps into a lifelong money strategy that multiplies over time.

Lesson 13 Learning Objectives

By the end of this lesson, you will be able to:

- Understand the core principles behind building long-term wealth using the cycle of saving, investing, and reinvesting.
- Set realistic monthly savings and investment goals to begin growing your money consistently.
- Use compound interest calculators to visualize how small, consistent investments grow over time.
- Identify income-generating opportunities through product or asset flipping.
- Create a personalized, repeatable strategy that turns income into wealth and keeps money in motion for growth.

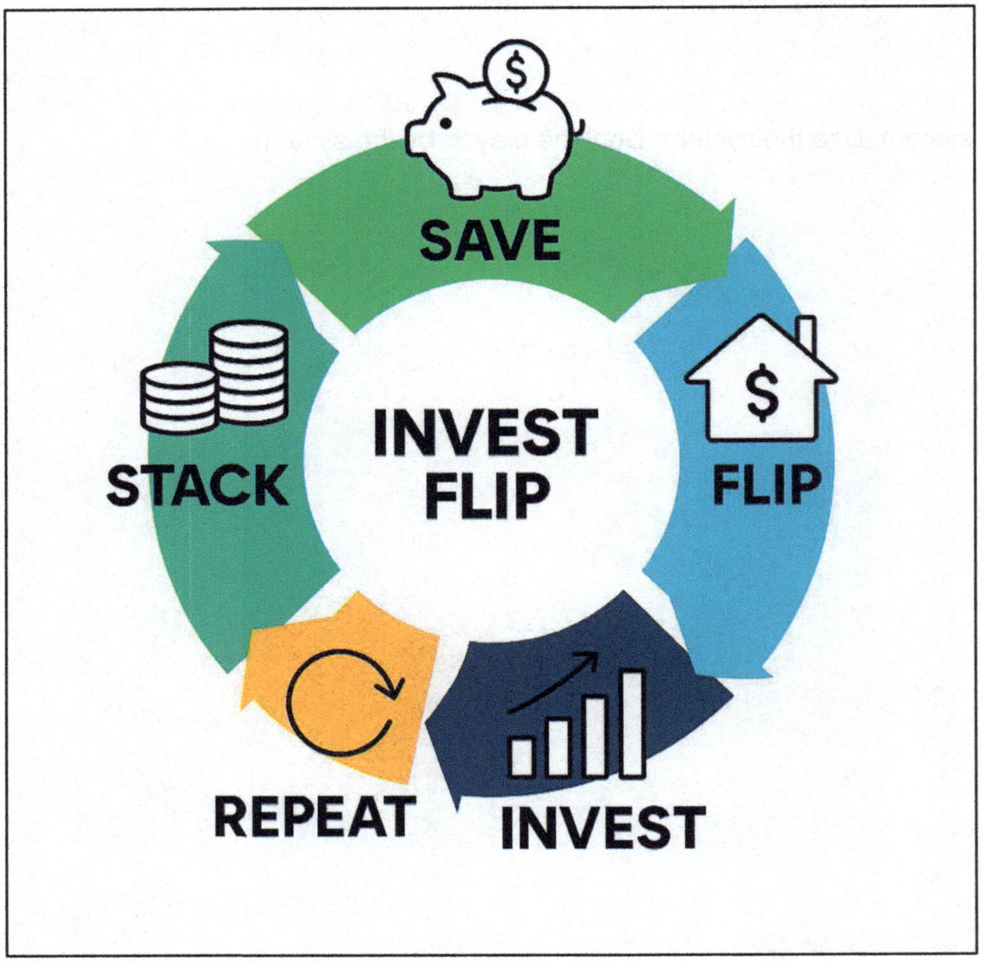

Exercise 13.1: Build Your Wealth Plan

1. Monthly Savings Goal: $____________

2. Monthly Investment Goal: $____________

3. First Investment Choice:

☐ Stocks/Index Funds
☐ Real Estate
☐ Small Business
☐ Other: ___________________

What's the first financial step you will take this month?

____

____

____

____

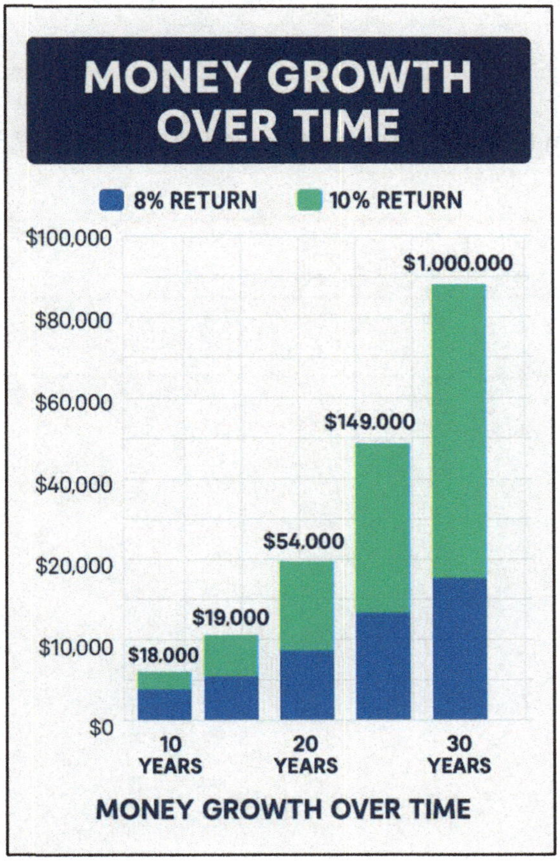

Exercise 13.2: Your Money Over Time

Use an online investment calculator (or app like Compound Interest Calculator).

Plug in: $100/month at 8% return.

Years	Investment Total	Future Value
10	$12,000	$18,294
20	$24,000	$49,423
30	$36,000	$122,346

Reflection:

What surprised you about these numbers?

____

____

____

____

What could you cut or earn to add $100/month to your investments?

____

____

____

Exercise 13.3: Find a Flip Opportunity

What's something you could flip (buy low, sell higher) to generate income?

- Product or Asset: ______________________________
- How much will it cost to start? $______________
- Where will you sell it? (eBay, local, IG, etc.): _______________________
- Estimated profit: $________________

Optional: Research and write down 2 websites or marketplaces where people are flipping this item successfully.

1. ____

2. ____

Final Takeaway

Wealth isn't magic—it's momentum. Stack smart moves. Take calculated risks. And keep reinvesting.

Key Rule

Make your money hustle as hard as you do—and never stop the cycle.

Lesson 14: Creating Multiple Streams of Income

Having one paycheck is not enough. Let's change that. This lesson helps you explore new income paths, choose the right fit, and start stacking streams—one at a time.

Lesson 14 Learning Objectives

By the end of this lesson, you will be able to:

- Understand the importance of building multiple income streams for financial stability and resilience.
- Differentiate between active income, semi-passive income, and fully passive income streams.
- Assess your current income portfolio and identify vulnerabilities from income concentration.
- Prioritize which income streams to build first based on resources, timeline, and strategic fit.
- Create a realistic income diversification roadmap showing when to launch each stream over 5 years.
- Understand how to balance time and resources across multiple income sources without burnout.

Exercise 14.1: Income Stream Audit

List all your current income sources and monthly amounts:

Income Source	Type (Job/Business/Investment)	Monthly Amount	Active or Passive?
		$	☐ Active ☐ Passive
		$	☐ Active ☐ Passive
		$	☐ Active ☐ Passive
		$	☐ Active ☐ Passive

Total Monthly Income: $____________

Primary Income Source: ____

What percentage of your total income comes from your primary source? ______%

Reflection:

If you lost your primary income source tomorrow, how long could you survive?

____

____

____

What does this tell you about your financial security?

____

____

____

Exercise 14.2: Income Diversification Strategy

Risk Assessment:

Based on your Income Stream Audit, how would you rate your current income risk?

☐ **High Risk** – 80%+ from one source
☐ **Medium Risk** – 50-79% from one source
☐ **Low Risk** – Income spread across 3+ sources

Income Stream Categories:

Which types of income do you currently have? (Check all that apply)

☐ Employment Income (W-2 job, salary)
☐ Business Income (side hustle, freelance, self-employment)
☐ Investment Income (stocks, real estate, dividends)

Diversification Plan:

Which 3 income stream types will you develop over the next 12 months?

1. ______________________________

Target start date: __________

2. ______________________________

Target start date: __________

3. ______________________________

Target start date: __________

How will you allocate your time across these streams?

____

____

____

____

What's your exit strategy? (When can you reduce or eliminate your primary income source?)

Exercise 14.3: Income Stream Priority Matrix

List 3-5 income stream ideas you're considering. Evaluate each one:

Income Stream Idea	Startup Difficulty (Low/Med/High)	Time to First Dollar (Days/Weeks/Months/Years)	Long-term Potential ($100/mo, $1K/mo, $10K+/mo)
Example: Freelance writing	Low	Weeks	$500-$2K/month
1.			
2.			
3.			
4.			
5.			

Based on this evaluation, which income stream should you build FIRST?

Why did you choose this one?

Which income stream will you build SECOND (after the first one is generating consistent income)?

What resource or skill do you need to develop before you can start your second stream?

Exercise 14.4: The 30-Day Income Stream Launch Plan

Use this checklist to stay on track as you turn your idea into income. Check off each step and keep notes on progress.

Income Stream I'm Launching: ____

(From Exercise 14.3 – the one you identified to build FIRST)

Week 1: Research & Setup (Days 1-7)

What accounts, tools, or resources do I need to set up?

What research do I need to do? (pricing, competitors, platforms)

Specific tasks I'll complete this week:

1.

2.

3.

Week 2: Prepare Your Offer (Days 8-14)

What exactly am I offering? (product/service description)

What's my pricing?

What materials do I need? (flyer, portfolio, samples, pitch)

Specific tasks I'll complete this week:

1.

2.

3.

Week 3: Soft Launch (Days 15-21)

Who are the first 10 people I'll tell about this?

1. ____________ 2. ____________ 3. ____________ 4. ____________ 5. ____________

2. ____________ 7. ____________ 8. ____________ 9. ____________ 10. ____________

Where will I promote it? (social media, groups, word of mouth)

First Sale Goal: Make $________ by Day 21

Specific tasks I'll complete this week:

1.

2.

3.

Week 4: Refine & Scale (Days 22-30)

What feedback did I get from my first customer(s)?

What do I need to improve?

How can I reach more people?

Specific tasks I'll complete this week:

1.

2.

3.

Accountability Partner:

Who will check in with me weekly to keep me on track?

Name: ________________________ Contact: ________________________

Exercise 14.5: 5-Year Income Stream Roadmap

Map out when you'll launch each income stream and what income you project from each:

Year 1: Foundation

Primary Income Stream: ____

Projected Monthly Income: $____________

New Stream Launching: ____

Projected Monthly Income by Year-End: $____________

Total Projected Monthly Income Year 1: $____________

Major Milestone: ____

Year 2: Growth

Streams Active:

1. ____ Monthly: $____________
2. ____ Monthly: $____________

New Stream Launching: ____

Projected Monthly Income by Year-End: $____________

Total Projected Monthly Income Year 2: $____________

Major Milestone: ____

Year 3: Diversification

Streams Active:

1. ____ Monthly: $____________
2. ____ Monthly: $____________
3. ____ Monthly: $____________

New Stream Launching (Passive): ____

Projected Monthly Income by Year-End: $____________

Total Projected Monthly Income Year 3: $____________

Major Milestone: ______________________________________

Year 4: Optimization

Streams Active:

1. ______________________________________ Monthly: $___________
2. ______________________________________ Monthly: $___________
3. ______________________________________ Monthly: $___________
4. ______________________________________ Monthly: $___________

Total Projected Monthly Income Year 4: $___________

Major Milestone: ______________________________________

Year 5: Financial Resilience

Streams Active:

1. ______________________________________ Monthly: $___________
2. ______________________________________ Monthly: $___________
3. ______________________________________ Monthly: $___________
4. ______________________________________ Monthly: $___________
5. ______________________________________ Monthly: $___________

Total Projected Monthly Income Year 5: $___________

Major Milestone: ______________________________________

Reinvestment Strategy:

Where will you reinvest income from your first streams to build new ones?

Long-Term Vision:

By Year 5, what will your income portfolio look like?

What kind of financial freedom will this give you?

Final Takeaway

Financial security isn't about having one big income—it's about having many small ones that add up to freedom. Don't wait for perfect conditions. Start stacking streams with what you have right now.

Key Rule

One income is risky. Multiple incomes = resilience, security, and peace of mind.

Lesson 15: Smart is the New Gangsta – Financial Intelligence

The real flex isn't fast money—it's knowing how to keep it, grow it, and protect it. Financial intelligence gives you the power to break cycles and build legacy.

Lesson 15 Learning Objectives

By the end of this lesson, you will be able to:

- Define your own "financial intelligence" based on skills learned throughout this course.
- Identify and replace limiting money behaviors with wealth-building habits.
- Create a personal 90-day learning plan to deepen financial knowledge in areas that still feel intimidating.
- Connect daily financial choices to long-term legacy goals.
- Articulate your financial identity and see yourself as a strategic wealth-builder, not just a hustler.

Exercise 15.1: My Financial Identity Map

Create a visual map of your financial life right now. Fill in each section with your current reality.

Income Streams (Lesson 14)

List all your current income sources:

1. ____ Monthly: $____________
2. ____ Monthly: $____________
3. ____ Monthly: $____________

Total Monthly Income: $____________

Monthly Expenses (Lesson 3)

Major expense categories:

- Housing: $____________
- Food: $____________
- Transportation: $____________
- Debt Payments: $____________
- Other: $____________

Total Monthly Expenses: $____________

Debts (Lesson 4)

List your current debts:

1. ______________________________ Balance: $____________
2. ______________________________ Balance: $____________
3. ______________________________ Balance: $____________

Total Debt: $____________

Assets (Lessons 7, 11)

What do you own that has value or generates income?

1. ______________________________ Value: $____________
2. ______________________________ Value: $____________
3. ______________________________ Value: $____________

Total Assets: $____________

Short-Term Goals (Lesson 1 - Next 6-12 months)

1. ____
2. ____
3. ____

Long-Term Goals (Lessons 9, 16 - 3-10 years)

1. ____
2. ____
3. ____

Legacy Vision (Lesson 9)

What do you want your money to accomplish for your family and community?

Reflection:

Looking at your complete financial map, where are you strongest?

Where do you need more strategy or focus?

POOR VS. WEALTHY MINDSET

Poor Mindset	Wealthy Mindset
✗ Money controls them	✓ They control money
✗ Pays themselves last	✓ Pays themselves first
✗ Live beyond their means	✓ Live below their means
✗ Fears change	✓ Adapts to change
✗ Spends to impress others	✓ Spends to build assets
✗ Avoids talking about money	✓ Openly discusses money
✗ Avoids talking about money	✓ Open ly discuss

Exercise 15.2: Money Script Rewrite

Old money belief: What's one limiting belief about money you inherited or developed?

____

____

Where did this belief come from? (Family, experience, culture etc.)

____

____

____

New empowered belief: Based on what you've learned in this course, write a new belief to replace the old one:

____

____

What evidence do you have that this new belief is true? (Reference lessons, actions you've taken, skills you've learned)

____

____

____

____

Commitment: How will you remind yourself of this new belief when the old one tries to come back?

____

____

____

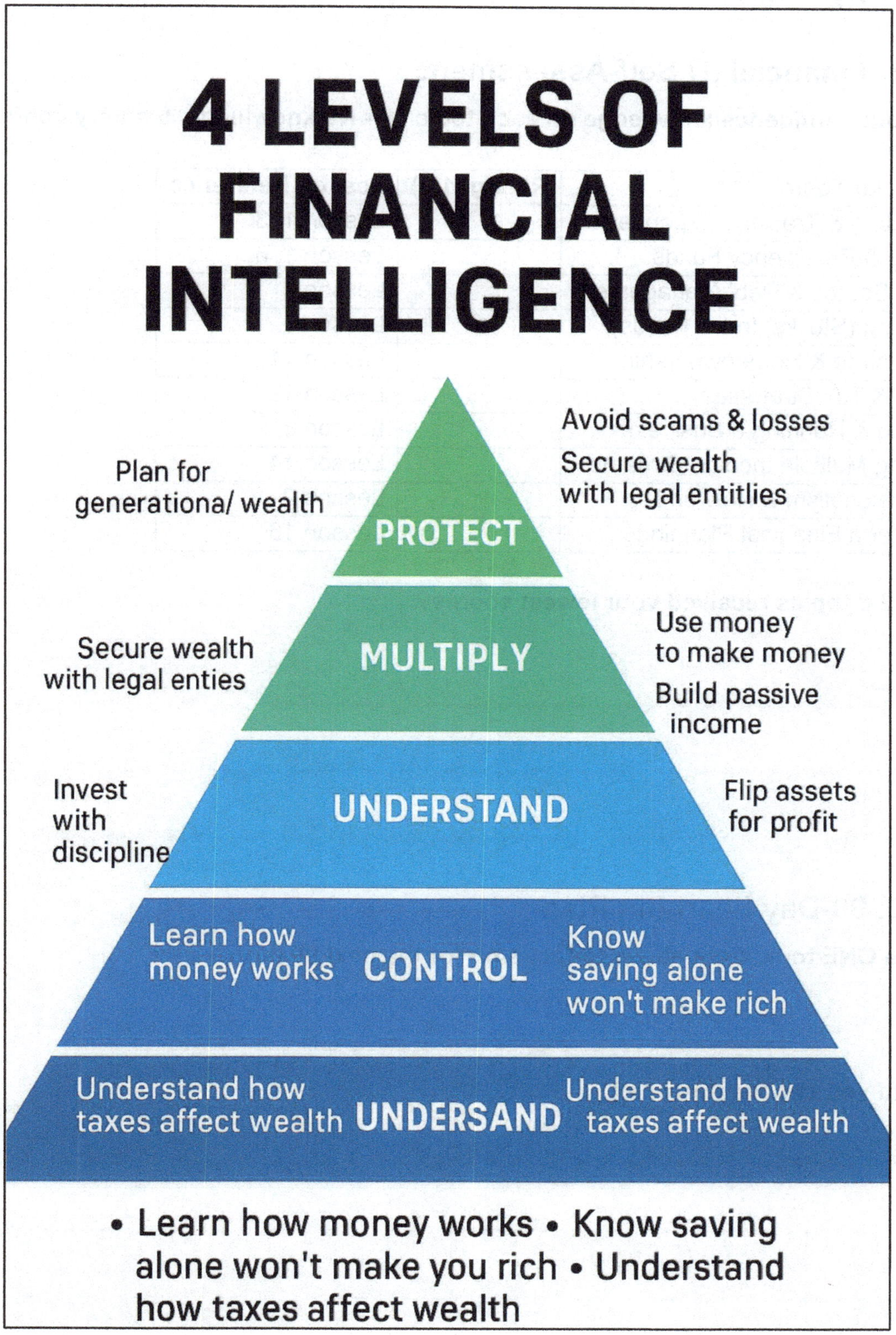
4 LEVELS OF FINANCIAL INTELLIGENCE
Avoid scams & losses
Secure wealth with legal entitlies
Plan for generationa/ wealth
PROTECT
Secure wealth with legal enties
MULTIPLY
Use money to make money
Build passive income
Invest with discipline
UNDERSTAND
Flip assets for profit
Learn how money works
CONTROL
Know saving alone won't make rich
Understand how taxes affect wealth
UNDERSAND
Understand how taxes affect wealth
• Learn how money works • Know saving alone won't make you rich • Understand how taxes affect wealth

Exercise 15.3: Financial IQ Self-Assessment & 90-Day Learning Plan

Part 1: Financial IQ Self-Assessment

Rate your confidence/knowledge on each topic (1 = No knowledge, 5 = Very confident):

Financial Topic	Rating (1-5)	Lesson Reference
Budgeting & Tracking Expenses		Lesson 1, 3
Saving & Emergency Funds		Lesson 1, 6
Credit Scores & Debt Management		Lesson 4
Investing (Stocks, Index Funds)		Lesson 7
Real Estate & Homeownership		Lesson 11
Taxes & Tax Strategies		Lesson 12
Starting & Running a Business		Lesson 8, 9
Building Multiple Income Streams		Lesson 14
Professionalism & Networking		Lesson 2
Long-term Financial Planning		Lesson 16

Which 2-3 topics received your lowest scores?

1. ______________________________

2. ______________________________

3. ______________________________

Part 2: 90-Day Learning Plan

Choose ONE topic from above to focus on for the next 90 days:

____

Why did you choose this one?

____

____

____

Find 3 Resources to Learn This Topic:

Resource 1 - Book:

Title: ____

When will you read it? ____

Resource 2 - Video/Course:

Platform/Channel: ____

When will you watch/complete it? ____

Resource 3 - Person to Ask:

Who knows about this topic that you can learn from?

Name: ____

When will you reach out? ____

Commitment: By the end of 90 days, what will you know or be able to do that you can't do now?

____

____

____

____

Recommended Resources by Topic:

- **Budgeting:** Apps (YNAB, Mint), Books (The Total Money Makeover)
- **Investing:** Books (The Simple Path to Wealth), YouTube (Minority Mindset, Graham Stephan)
- **Real Estate:** Books (The Book on Rental Property Investing), Podcasts (BiggerPockets)
- **Taxes:** IRS.gov Free File, YouTube (ClearValue Tax), Local VITA programs
- **Business:** Books (The $100 Startup), Courses (Skillshare, Coursera)
- **Credit:** AnnualCreditReport.com, YouTube (The Credit Pros), Books (Your Score)

Exercise 15.4: Legacy Letter

Write a letter to your future self, your children, or your family about the financial legacy you're building.

Use these prompts to guide you:

- What do you want your money to accomplish in 10 years?
- What do you want your children/family to say about you and money?
- What impact do you want to have on your community?
- What financial legacy are you committed to leaving?

Dear ______________________________________,

With commitment and vision,

Name: ____________________________________

Date: ____________________________________

Reflection:

What emotions came up while writing this letter?

What's one daily financial choice you can make that aligns with this legacy vision?

Final Takeaway

Financial intelligence isn't just about knowing the rules—it's about knowing yourself, your purpose, and your power. You now have the knowledge. The question is: What will you do with it?

Key Rule

Smart is the new gangsta. Knowledge + strategy + action = generational wealth.

Lesson 16: Financial Freedom Planning

Financial freedom isn't just about money—it's about choice. It's waking up every day knowing you own your time, not your bills.

Lesson 16 Learning Objectives

By the end of this lesson, you will be able to:

- Define financial freedom and differentiate between stability, independence, and abundance.
- Calculate your personal "freedom number" — the amount of passive income needed to cover monthly living expenses.
- Identify and evaluate income-generating assets such as real estate, investments, and business ventures.
- Develop a basic 5-year financial freedom plan, including savings, investing, and passive income strategies.
- Commit to one action step toward replacing earned income with asset-driven income.

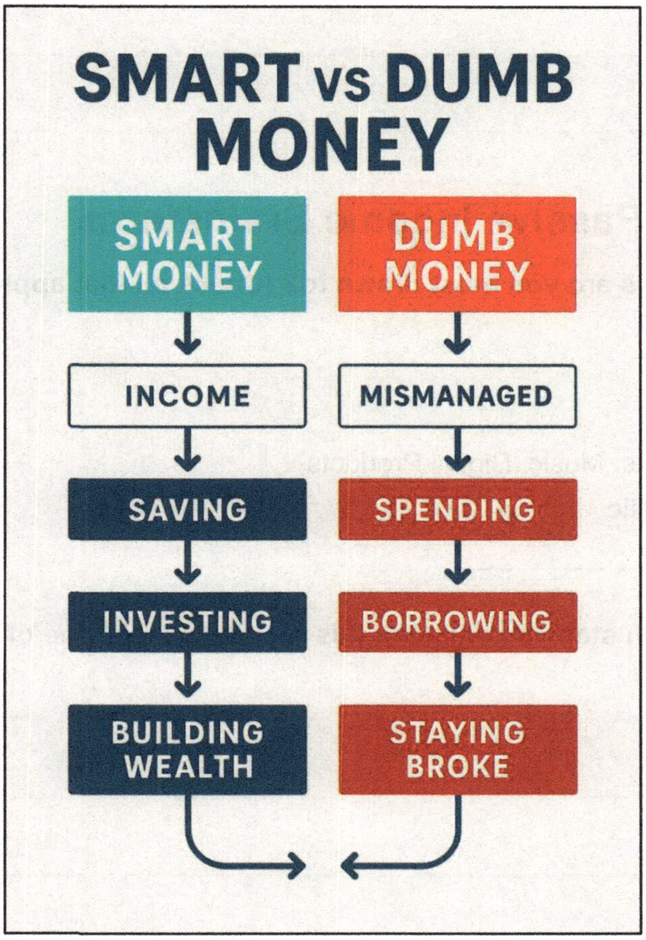

Exercise 16.1: Financial Freedom Number Calculation

Step 1: What are your current monthly living expenses?

$______________________

Step 2: How much monthly passive income would you need to stop working a 9–5 job?

$______________________

Step 3: Freedom number = Monthly passive income needed

How does this number compare to what you're earning now?

____

____

____

____

____

____

Exercise 16.2: Passive Income Brainstorm

Which income streams are you most drawn to? (Check all that apply)

☐ Real Estate

☐ Stocks/Dividends

☐ Online Business

☐ Royalties (e.g., Books, Music, Digital Products)

☐ Automated Side Hustle

☐ Other: ______________________

What is the first action step you will take this month to build one of these?

____

____

____

____

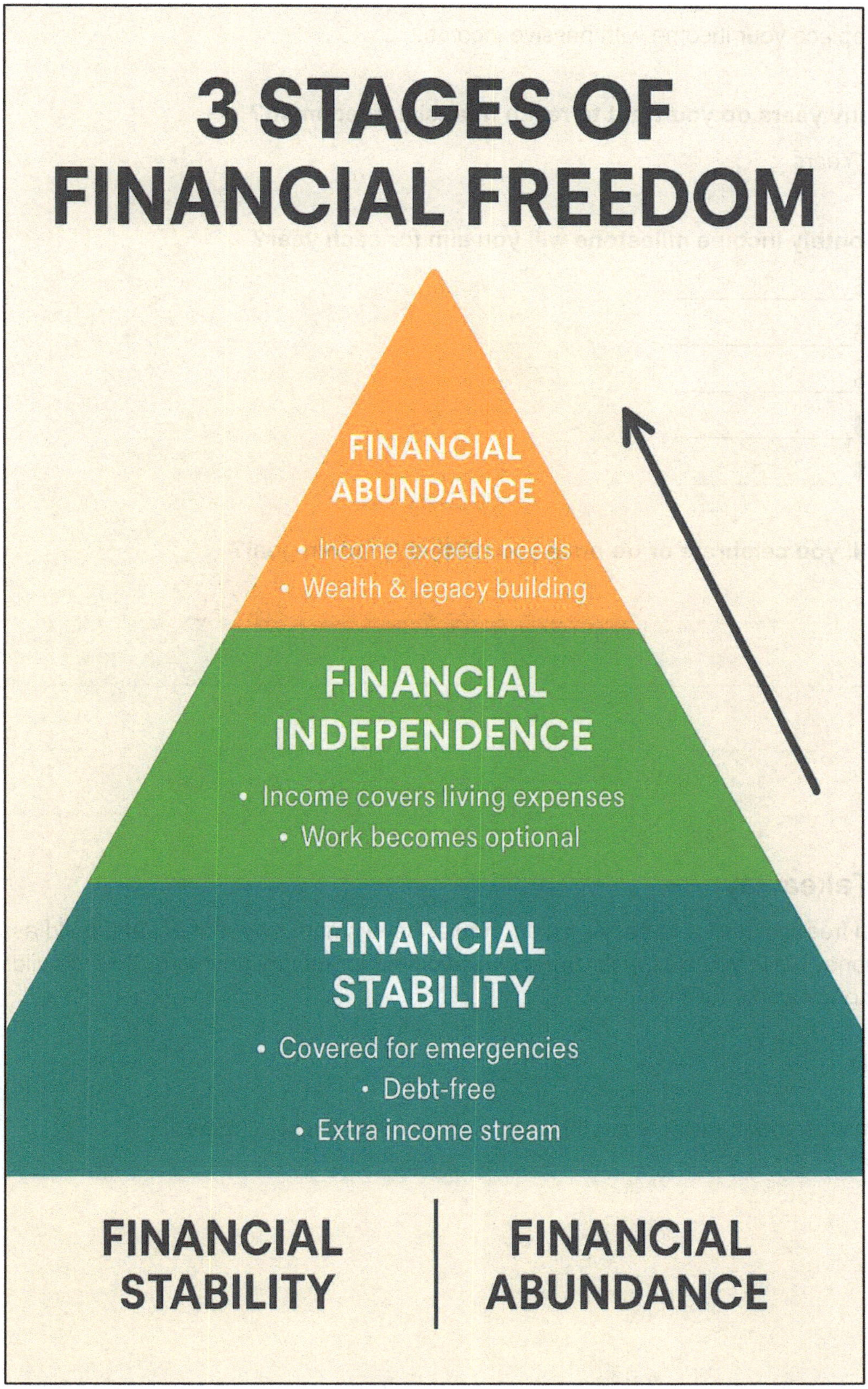
3 STAGES OF FINANCIAL FREEDOM
FINANCIAL ABUNDANCE
• Income exceeds needs
• Wealth & legacy building
FINANCIAL INDEPENDENCE
• Income covers living expenses
• Work becomes optional
FINANCIAL STABILITY
• Covered for emergencies
• Debt-free
• Extra income stream
FINANCIAL STABILITY
FINANCIAL ABUNDANCE

Exercise 16.3: Financial Freedom Timeline

Goal: Replace your income with passive income.

How many years do you want to reach financial freedom in?

______ Years

What monthly income milestone will you aim for each year?

Year 1: $____________

Year 2: $____________

Year 3: $____________

Year 4: $____________

Year 5: $____________

What will you celebrate or do once you hit that freedom goal?

____

____

____

____

Final Takeaway

Financial freedom isn't a fantasy—it's a formula. Save smart, invest often, and build assets that make money while you sleep. You're not just working for money anymore. You're building a life where money works for YOU.

Key Rule

Freedom isn't about having everything—it's about controlling your time.

Lesson 17: Wrap-Up & Action Steps

You've made it through the blueprint. Now it's time to turn your knowledge into power—and your power into action.

Lesson 17 Learning Objectives

By the end of this lesson, you will be able to:

- Reflect on and summarize key financial concepts and skills learned throughout the course.
- Identify and write short-, mid-, and long-term financial goals using clear, actionable steps.
- Create a 12-month financial challenge plan to apply knowledge in real life and track monthly progress.
- Make a personal commitment to continued financial growth and identify accountability partners for support.
- Understand that consistency and action—not perfection—are the foundation for lifelong financial success.

Exercise 17.1: Financial Goal-Setting Plan

Short-Term Goal (1 year):

____

____

Mid-Term Goal (5 years):

____

____

____

Long-Term Goal (10+ years):

____

____

____

What daily habit will support these goals?

What weekly habit will support these goals?

What monthly habit will support these goals?

Exercise 17.2: The 12-Month Money Challenge

Write down one goal per month that will move your finances forward.

Month	Financial Goal	Completed?
Jan		☐
Feb		☐
Mar		☐
Apr		☐
May		☐
Jun		☐
Jul		☐
Aug		☐
Sep		☐
Oct		☐
Nov		☐
Dec		☐

Ideas: Save $1,000, open a stock account, create a side hustle, pay off credit card, etc.

Exercise 17.3: Financial Success Commitment

Finish this sentence: "I commit to building wealth by…"

Accountability Partners: Write down 3 people or groups who will keep you motivated and on track:

1. ______

2. ______

3. ______

Final Takeaway

"The greatest wealth-building tool is not money—it's knowledge backed by consistent action." You now hold the keys. Now go unlock your future.

Keep saving. Keep investing. Keep building.

Key Rule

This isn't the end. This is the beginning of a smarter, freer, more powerful money life.

Closing Statement from the Author — Dory Laramore

If you've made it to this point, then you've taken the first real step toward changing your financial future. This isn't just another workbook—it's a blueprint, a game plan, a roadmap to breaking cycles and building something real. And if nobody ever told you before, let me be the first to say it: YOU DESERVE FINANCIAL FREEDOM.

I know what it's like to come from nothing, to feel like the odds are stacked against you, to believe that wealth is something only "other people" have access to. That's a lie. The truth is, the system wasn't built to teach us this game, but that doesn't mean we can't master it. The same mindset that got you through struggle—the hustle, the discipline, the ability to adapt—is the same mindset that will get you to financial success.

No matter where you are right now, you are not stuck. No matter what mistakes you've made, you are not disqualified. The only thing standing between where you are and where you want to be is consistent action and smart decisions.

Now that you have the knowledge, what will you do with it?

I challenge you to apply what you've learned, to take real steps toward saving, investing, starting a business, and growing your money the right way. Do it for yourself. Do it for your family. Do it for the next generation so they never have to start from scratch like we did.

This isn't the end of the journey—it's just the beginning. Stay hungry, stay disciplined, and never stop leveling up.

I'll see you at the top.

Let's build. Let's grow. Let's win.

— Dory Laramore

Glossary: Basic Financial Terms

Asset – Something you own that has value, like cash, a car, a house, or shares in a business.

Bear Market – A period when investment prices are generally falling, and people are cautious or pessimistic.

Bond – A loan you give to a company or government. They promise to pay you back with interest over time.

Budget – A plan for how you will spend and save your money each month.

Bull Market – A period when investment prices are generally rising, and people are optimistic.

Capital – Money used to start an investment or grow a business.

Capital Gains – The profit you make when you sell an investment for more than you paid for it.

Compound Interest – Earning interest not only on your original money but also on the interest it has already earned. This is how money grows over time.

Credit – Your ability to borrow money with the promise to pay it back later.

Credit Score – A number that tells lenders how trustworthy you are with borrowed money, based on your financial history.

Debt – Money you owe to someone else, like a student loan, mortgage, or credit card balance.

Deduction (Tax) – An expense (like mortgage interest or charitable donations) you can subtract from your income to lower the amount of tax you owe.

Diversification – The strategy of spreading your money across different types of investments to reduce risk. Often called "not putting all your eggs in one basket."

Dividend – A payment some companies make to their shareholders (stock owners) from their profits.

Dollar-Cost Averaging – Investing a fixed amount of money on a regular schedule (like $100 every month), regardless of whether prices are up or down. This removes emotion from investing.

Emergency Fund – Savings set aside specifically for unexpected expenses, like a car repair or medical bill.

ETF (Exchange-Traded Fund) – A bundle of investments (like stocks or bonds) that you can buy and sell like a single stock. It's an easy way to diversify.

Expenses – The money you spend on needs and wants, like rent, food, utilities, and entertainment.

Income – Money you earn from sources like a job, a business, a side hustle, or investments.

Index Fund – A type of investment that automatically buys shares of all the companies in a specific market index (like the S&P 500). It's a simple, low-cost way to invest in the whole market.

Interest – The cost of borrowing money (what you pay on a loan) or the reward for saving/investing (what you earn in a savings account).

Investment – Using your money to buy something (like stocks, bonds, or property) with the goal of making it grow over time.

Liability – Something that takes money out of your pocket, like a car loan, credit card debt, or a mortgage.

Net Worth – A snapshot of your financial health. It's calculated by subtracting everything you owe (liabilities) from everything you own (assets).

Passive Income – Money you earn with little daily effort after the initial work is done. Examples include rental income, royalties, or dividends.

Portfolio – Your personal collection of all your investments (stocks, bonds, funds, etc.).

Principal – The original amount of money you invest or borrow, not including any interest or earnings.

Return on Investment (ROI) – A measure of your profit or loss. It tells you how much money you made (or lost) on an investment compared to what you put in.

Risk Tolerance – How comfortable you are with the possibility of losing money on an investment in exchange for the potential to earn more.

Savings Account – A bank account designed to hold your money safely while earning a small amount of interest.

Side Hustle – A way to make extra money outside of your main job.

Stock – A share of ownership in a company. If the company does well, the value of your share can increase.

Tax Credit – A dollar-for-dollar reduction in the amount of tax you owe. It's more valuable than a tax deduction.

Time Horizon – The length of time you plan to keep your money invested before you need to use it (e.g., for a house in 5 years or retirement in 30 years).

Wealth – The total value of everything you own (your assets). True wealth is built by owning assets that grow or generate income over time.